Water Worlds

Coral Reefs

Cheryl Hook
for the Australian Museum

This edition first published in 2002 in the United States of America by Chelsea House Publishers, a subsidiary of Haights Cross Communications

Chelsea House Publishers
1974 Sproul Road, Suite 400
Broomall, PA 19008–0914

The Chelsea House world wide web address is www.chelseahouse.com

Library of Congress Cataloging-in-Publication Data Applied for.
ISBN 0-7910-6567-7

First published in 2000 by
Macmillan Education Australia Pty Ltd
627 Chapel Street, South Yarra, Australia, 3141

Copyright © Australian Museum 2000

Australian Museum Series Editor: Carolyn MacLulich
Australian Museum Scientific Adviser: Doug Hoese
Australian Museum Publishing Unit: Jenny Saunders and Kate Lowe

Edited by Anne McKenna
Typeset in Bembo
Printed in Hong Kong
Text and cover design by Leigh Ashforth @ watershed art & design
Illustrations by Peter Mather

Acknowledgements

For my daughter Lauren, who loves to snorkel

The author and publishers are grateful to the following for permission to use copyright material:

Front cover:
    Main photo: Mark Spencer/AUSCAPE
    Inset photo: R. & V. Taylor/Nature Focus
Back cover: Kevin Deacon/AUSCAPE

Becca Saunders/AUSCAPE, pp. 7 (top right), 25 (top); Cherie Vasas/Nature Travel and Marine Images, p. 14; D. Parer & E. Parer-Cook/AUSCAPE, pp. 13, 17 (top left), 18, 30; David B. Fleetham/OSF/AUSCAPE, p. 22 (bottom); G. Saueracker, p. 8; Jean-Paul Ferrero/AUSCAPE, pp. 17 (top right), 24; Jean-Marc La Roque/ AUSCAPE, p. 15 (bottom); Jiri Lochman/Lochman Transparencies, p. 21; John Cancalosi/AUSCAPE, p. 19; Kathie Atkinson pp. 7 (left), 11, 15 (top), 17 (bottom), 20, 23, 25 (bottom), 26; Kevin Deacon/AUSCAPE, pp. 4-5, 9, 10; M. McCoy/Nature Focus, p. 28; Mark Spencer/AUSCAPE, pp. 6, 7 (bottom right), 29 (top and bottom); R. & V. Taylor/Nature Focus, pp. 3, 16, 22 (top), 27.

Contents

What are coral reefs?

Coral reefs are living communities of animals and plants that live on, in and around underwater chains of rocks. The rocks of coral reefs are made from millions of broken skeletons of dead sea animals that have become stuck together. Most of the skeletons come from small animals called **coral polyps**.

Many different sorts of corals live over the rocks that form the base of coral reefs.

Coral reefs are found in clear, warm, shallow water in tropical **oceans**. Some coral reefs form on **continental shelves** close to land. Other coral reefs form around the edges of islands in the middle of deep oceans.

All coral reefs are slightly different to each other. However, coral reefs do have things in common and can be divided into different parts. Each part has its own special features.

Coral reefs are home to a huge variety of animals and plants. Animals and plants breed, grow, feed and live their whole lives as parts of big communities that live on, in and around coral reefs. Some groups of animals and plants only live in particular parts of coral reefs, such as coral flats. Other groups of animals and plants live over the whole coral reef area. One example is fishes that swim in and out of coral reefs with rising and falling tides.

Coral reefs are important to people because they are special places. Many people visit coral reefs because they are so beautiful. Some people study coral reefs and their living communities because they want to find out more about these amazing places.

Thousands of fishes swim in and out of coral reefs with rising and falling tides.

≋ This is a coral garden. It shows the great variety of animals and plants that live in, on and around coral reefs.

Did you know?
The word 'reef' comes from an old Viking word 'rif', which means rib.

Coral polyps

Coral polyps are animals. They are related to anemones and jellyfish. Like anemones and jellyfish, coral polyps have soft, jelly-like bodies with sets of stinging tentacles around their mouths. They range in size from a fraction of an inch to several inches. Some coral polyps live alone, but most form large groups called colonies.

Types of coral polyps

Coral polyps are divided into two groups. One group, called **hard corals** or reef builders, has skeletons. The other group, called **soft corals**, does not have skeletons.

Hard corals

Hard corals have a bony skeleton on the outside of their bodies. Their skeleton is made from a hard material called calcium carbonate and is shaped like a cup. The skeleton helps to protect the soft bodies of coral polyps from being eaten by other animals or being damaged by waves. During the day, most coral polyps hide inside their skeletons and only come out at night to feed.

Did you know?
Coral polyps that live in colonies are all connected together by their stomachs.

≋ Hard corals grow in many different shapes and sizes.

Some hard corals, such as plate corals, grow flat.

Other hard corals, such as staghorn corals, grow 'branches'.

Soft corals

Soft corals do not have bony skeletons. Instead, some have tiny **limestone** needles called spicules inside their soft bodies that help to protect them. However, most soft corals protect themselves by producing poisonous chemicals. The chemicals make them taste so bad that most animals will not eat them.

Unlike hard corals, some soft corals are able to move. They kill nearby hard corals by putting poisonous chemicals into the water. The soft corals move in and take the hard corals' place. However, soft corals are unlikely to take over the entire reef, as they tend to get damaged easily by storms.

≋ This photo shows the spicules and tentacles on one type of soft coral.

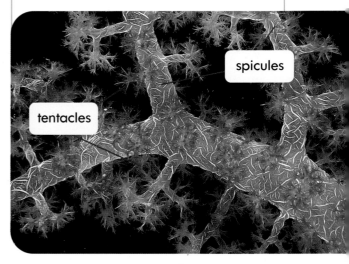

spicules

tentacles

≋ A close-up view of soft coral polyps.

Sets of tentacles

Coral polyps eat and get rid of their wastes through their mouths.

This is the body of a soft coral polyp. It does not have a bony skeleton around it.

≋ Soft corals are easily damaged so they tend to grow best in sheltered parts of coral reefs.

How coral polyps reproduce

Coral polyps can reproduce in two ways. One way is called **asexual reproduction** and the other is called **sexual reproduction**.

Asexual reproduction

In asexual reproduction, an adult coral polyp divides into two new coral polyps. This is called budding. Other animals such as starfish are also able to do this, but usually to replace lost body parts rather than to make a whole new starfish.

≋ Blue Sea Stars live on reefs. This one is shown budding from its centre.

≋ These staghorn corals are releasing hundreds of bundles of sperm and eggs into the water. Sometimes the water has so many bundles of eggs and sperm floating in it that divers say it is like swimming through snow.

Sexual reproduction

In sexual reproduction, a female egg and a male sperm must join together to make a new coral polyp.

Some coral polyps make both eggs and sperm inside their own bodies. They are able to reproduce on their own. Animals that are able to do this are called **hermaphrodites** (say: her-maf-ro-dites).

Other coral polyps only make either eggs or sperm. Because coral polyps are not able to move about and find a partner, they must have a way to join their eggs and sperm together. So on certain nights of the year, coral polyps release small bundles of eggs and sperm at the same time. This is called mass spawning.

The bundles float to the sea surface and break open. The eggs and sperm then mix together and, if an egg and a sperm from the same sort of coral combine, a new coral polyp will grow.

How coral polyps find food

Coral polyps find food in two ways. Firstly, they catch food during the night and secondly, they use tiny plants growing inside them to make food during the day.

During the night, most coral polyps feed by stretching out their stinging tentacles and catching tiny floating animals from the sea water around them. The food is then passed into their mouth and down into their stomachs. Because most coral polyps are connected to each other by their stomachs, they all share any food caught.

During the day, some coral polyps use tiny plants inside their bodies called **zooxanthellae** (say: zoo-an-the-lee) to make food. Zooxanthellae use sunlight to change **nutrients** from the sea water into food for the coral polyps. They also help coral polyps build their skeletons by making calcium carbonate.

What eats corals?

Poisonous soft corals are eaten by animals called egg cowries. Egg cowries use juices in their **guts** to change the poison of soft corals into a harmless chemical.

Crown of Thorns Starfish

Crown of Thorns Starfish eat soft corals but seem to like hard corals better. They are able to eat hard corals by breaking them down with stomach juices. First, the starfish move onto an area of hard corals. Then they pull their stomach out through their mouths. Next, they spill stomach juices all over the hard coral polyps. Their stomach juices are strong enough to kill the coral polyps. The polyps break down and become a kind of polyp soup. Finally, the starfish suck the soup through their mouths. If large numbers of Crown of Thorns Starfish feed at the same time, they can kill big patches of coral reefs.

The Crown of Thorns Starfish is feeding on a type of hard coral.

The white patch is dead coral. The starfish has eaten all the living coral polyps.

How coral reefs are built

Coral reefs take many years to build. They are built mostly from skeletons of hard corals mixed with sand and the remains of other plants and animals. When hard corals die, their bony skeletons are left behind. Over many years, millions of their skeletons build up. Eventually, they all become stuck together and form hard rock. The rock is called limestone. The limestone then forms a platform for new coral polyps to grow on.

≋ The color of hard corals comes from tiny patches in the skin of coral polyps. When they die and their skin rots away, a white bony skeleton is left behind. Other sea animals that are like hard corals have red, blue or other brightly colored skeletons. They are not proper corals but distant relatives.

Did you know?
Scientists have drilled into coral reefs and found the limestone to be 200 meters (656 feet) thick in parts.

Where coral reefs are found

Most coral reefs are found in tropical areas where sea water is warm, shallow and clean.

Hard corals will only grow in warm water. The water temperature needs to be about the same as a lukewarm bath—between 20 and 30 degrees Celsius (68° and 86° F).

Hard corals use sunlight to make food. So most hard corals grow in areas where the sunlight can pass through the water. These waters are less than 60 meters (200 feet) deep.

Clean water allows the most light to reach hard corals. If the water is dirty, light is unable to get to the hard corals. Hard corals then die because they cannot make enough food to survive.

≋ This map shows that coral reefs are found in tropical areas.

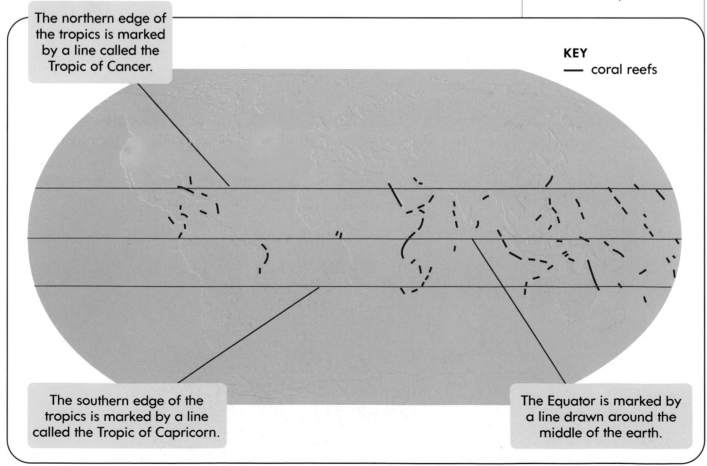

The northern edge of the tropics is marked by a line called the Tropic of Cancer.

KEY
— coral reefs

The southern edge of the tropics is marked by a line called the Tropic of Capricorn.

The Equator is marked by a line drawn around the middle of the earth.

The tropics

Oceans are warmest in the **tropics**. The tropics are areas of land and sea that lie on either side of the **Equator**. The Equator is the part of the world where the sun is always directly above you at midday. On a world map, the Equator and the tropics are marked by lines that run across the Earth. Places between these lines generally have very hot weather. Hot weather makes the water in the oceans very warm too.

The biggest coral reef

The biggest coral reef in the world is the Great Barrier Reef, which lies off the coast of eastern Queensland, Australia. It is made up of nearly 3,000 different coral reefs and islands. The Great Barrier Reef covers an area of more than 350,000 square kilometers (136,500 square miles), which is bigger than Great Britain or the Australian state of Victoria, and about half the size of the state of Texas in the United States of America.

≋ Part of the Great Barrier Reef

Did you know?
Astronauts in space can see the outline of the Great Barrier Reef when they look down at the Earth.

Types of coral reefs

There are many different types of coral reefs in tropical oceans. Coral reefs that form in similar ways are grouped together and given special names. There are three types of coral reefs:

- **Fringing reefs** form on continental shelves close to the mainland or around the edges of islands that were once joined to the mainland.
- **Barrier reefs** form on the edges of continental shelves and make a barrier between the mainland and deeper parts of the ocean.
- **Atolls** form in the middle of deep oceans.

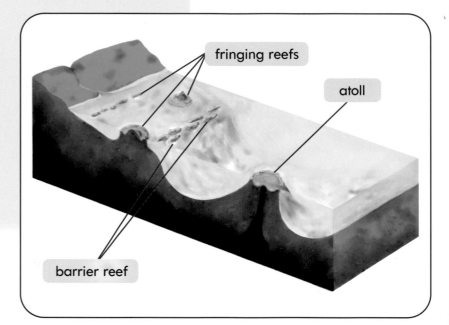

Fringing reefs

Fringing reefs form on parts of the sea-bed called the continental shelf. The continental shelf lies next to the mainland and is covered by shallow water. Fringing reefs also form around the edges of **continental islands**. Continental islands are the tops of hills or mountains that were once part of the mainland but became cut off as sea levels rose.

≋ Some fringing reefs form close to the mainland.

Barrier reefs

Barrier reefs form on parts of continental shelves well away from the mainland. They are made up of many different **cays**, fringing reefs and lagoons. Together they create a barrier between the mainland and deeper parts of the ocean.

≋ In this picture you can see part of the Great Barrier Reef. The light blue water is very shallow, but the dark blue water in the distance is deep.

Atolls

Coral reefs that form in the shape of a ring or horseshoe with a shallow area of water (called a lagoon) in the middle are called atolls. Most atolls are in the middle of tropical oceans where water is very deep. Some scientists think that atolls first form as fringing reefs around the edges of islands made by volcanoes. As sea levels rise, the volcanic islands are covered by sea water, leaving the coral reefs to keep growing in a ring shape.

≋ This picture shows part of the ring shape formed by atolls.

The shallow lagoon is inside the ring of coral.

Parts of coral reefs

Coral reefs are made up of different parts. Each part has special things about it, such as where it is or how it looks, which make it different to other parts of the reef. The diagram below shows a coral reef and its parts. Each part has its own name and special features.

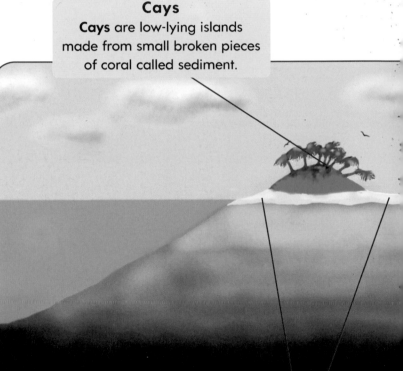

Cays
Cays are low-lying islands made from small broken pieces of coral called sediment.

Beaches
Beaches are strips of land lying next to the sea. They can be either sandy or rocky.

≋ These people are exploring reef flats at high tide.

≋ This cay has a sandy beach.

≋ The boulder zone has large dead coral boulders that are easy to see at low tide. The reef flat at low tide looks very muddy.

Reef crests
Reef crests are smooth, flat zones between boulder zones and reef edges.

Reef edges
Reef edges are where coral reefs finish and open oceans begin.

≋ The water in the open ocean is deep and looks dark blue.

Reef flats
Reef flats are flat areas lying off beaches. They are made up of sand, pieces of broken coral and large coral boulders that may be either dead or alive.

Boulder zones
Boulder zones are usually beyond reef flats. They are areas of large dead coral boulders.

Cays

Cays are low-lying islands that form in sheltered parts of coral reefs. They are made from bits of broken and ground-up pieces of coral called sediments. When sediments start to build up they form small sandbanks. Small sandbanks are unstable, which means that wind and waves can change or even destroy them. However, as time passes, more sediment is added to the sandbanks and they become bigger and more stable. Eventually, the sandbanks become so big, wide and high that they form cays.

≋ Large trees called screw pines grow on cays. Screw pines have special roots that help to hold them firmly in the ground.

Plants and animals

When cays first form they have very few animals and no plants living on them. The first animals to live on cays are shellfish and crabs. They get their food from the sediments that make cays. Seabirds fly to cays. Other animals, such as turtles, swim there. These animals only use cays as nesting places and get their food mainly from the sea.

Plant seeds get to cays in many different ways. Some seeds, such as coconut seeds, are washed in by sea currents. Other seeds, such as grass seeds, are blown by the wind. Many seeds are brought on birds' feathers or in birds' droppings.

To begin with, only small plants that grow in windy, salty places take root on cays. After a while, soil develops. The soil is made from dead plants and birds' droppings. Once soil forms and becomes deeper, larger plants, such as shrubs and trees, are able to grow.

Seabirds

Seabirds visit cays for a variety of reasons. Sometimes they stop at cays to rest when they are flying from one place to another. Occasionally, seabirds will visit cays when they are out hunting for food. Most often, seabirds visit cays to nest and lay their eggs. While some birds, such as herons, form big breeding colonies, other birds nest in small groups. Boobies nest on beaches, while tropic birds and frigate birds nest in trees and shrubs.

≋ Male frigate birds have a large red piece of skin on their neck. They blow up this piece of skin like a balloon when they want to mate with females.

Did you know?
Some **indigenous** Australians weave bags using leaves from the screw pine.

Beaches on cays

Beaches on cays are mostly made from the skeletons of dead animals such as hard corals, shellfish and fish. When sea animals die, their skeletons are broken into different sized pieces by waves. The pieces are washed onto sheltered parts of coral reefs and build up to form cays and cay beaches. There are two main types of beaches on cays:

- sandy beaches;
- rocky beaches.

The dark colored rock is beach rock made from sand grains that have become stuck together.

Sandy beaches

Sandy beaches are made from loose pieces of broken skeletons. There are three types of sandy beaches. Each type is made from different sized pieces.

- *Sand beaches* are made from pieces smaller than a pin head. They are called sand grains.
- *Shingle beaches* are made from pieces about the size of your little finger.
- *Rubble beaches* are made from pieces about the size of your index finger.

Rocky beaches

Rocky beaches are made from pieces of broken skeletons that have become stuck together. There are two types of rocky beaches. Each type is held together by a different 'glue'.

- *Beach rock beaches* are made when sand grains become stuck together by chemicals in the sand grains.
- *Cay rock beaches* are made when sand grains become stuck together by chemicals from birds' droppings.

≋ A sandy beach is made from tiny grains of broken shell and coral.

A female Green Turtle is making a hollow in the sand before laying her eggs.

Did you know?

*Cay rock is mined and turned into plant **fertilizer** because it is rich in a chemical called phosphate (say: fos-fait), which is good for plant growth.*

Turtles

Female turtles visit sandy beaches on cays to lay their eggs between October and February. First, female turtles make a hollow in the sand using their front flippers. Next, they lay between 50 and 150 eggs inside the hollow. The eggs look like ping-pong balls. They are round and have soft shells. Then, the turtles fill in the hollow with sand. If the eggs are buried deep under the sand where it is cool, mostly female turtles hatch. If the eggs are buried close to the surface of the sand where it is hot, mostly male turtles hatch. Finally, the female turtles go back to the sea, leaving their eggs alone. After six or seven weeks, the baby turtles dig their way out of the sand and head for the sea. Many young turtles are eaten by other animals before they become adults.

≋ Many baby turtles are eaten by other animals. If baby turtles hatch during the day, some will be eaten by waiting seabirds. If baby turtles hatch during the night, some will be eaten by crabs. This baby turtle has been caught by a Golden Ghost Crab.

Reef flats

Reef flats are parts of coral reefs. They lie close to beaches. Reef flats are made up of stretches of sand, pieces of broken coral and large coral boulders that may be either dead or alive. Reef flats can be quite large and are sometimes divided into two parts: inner reef flats, which are the closest reef flats to beaches; and outer reef flats, which are the closest reef flats to reef crests.

≋ Reef flats are good places to explore but they are easily damaged. Groups of visitors can cause more damage to them in one day than a bad storm.

Fishes on coral reefs

More types of fishes live on or around coral reefs than anywhere else in the oceans. Scientists think that there are about 15,000 different types of saltwater fishes in the world. They think that 7,000 different types of fishes live on or near coral reefs.

Parrotfishes

Parrotfishes are very brightly colored reef fishes. They have unusual teeth shaped like parrots' beaks. They use their teeth to scrape seaweed off coral reef boulders.

≋ At night, parrotfishes sleep in a slimy covering they make around their bodies.

Sea cucumbers

Some types of sea cucumbers have small see-through fishes called Pearl Fish living inside them. The fishes get inside sea cucumbers by wriggling tail-first through the sea cucumber's anus. Once inside, the fishes eat part of the sea cucumber's gut. This does not seem to harm the sea cucumber!

Food webs

Food webs show what different plants and animals eat and how their feeding patterns link with each other. In a food web, arrows point from the food to the living thing that eats it.

The feathery feeding parts of the sea cucumber search for drifting food.

≋ Sea cucumbers are like living vacuum cleaners. They feed on the sandy floors of reef flats. First, the sea cucumber sucks sand in through its mouth. Then, its gut takes in food from the sand. Finally, the sea cucumber passes the sand out through its anus. Its droppings look like little curly tubes of sand.

≋ A food web of a coral reef.

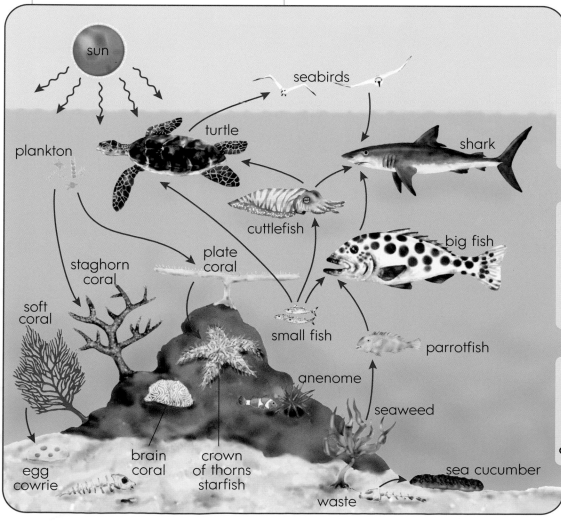

sun

seabirds

shark

turtle

plankton

cuttlefish

big fish

staghorn coral

plate coral

soft coral

small fish

parrotfish

anenome

seaweed

egg cowrie

brain coral

crown of thorns starfish

sea cucumber

waste

Carnivores (say: kar-ni-vorz) are living things that eat other animals. For example, sharks eat parrotfish.

Herbivores (say: her-bi-vorz) are living things that eat plants. For example, parrotfish eat seaweeds.

Plants are the beginning of all food webs. One group of plants that live in oceans are seaweeds.

Boulder zones

Boulder zones are parts of coral reefs. In some coral reefs, the reef flats blend into an area of slightly higher ground before the reef crests. These are called boulder zones. Boulder zones are made up of large dead coral boulders. The boulders are usually covered in brightly colored seaweeds and other plants. Even though boulder zones look dead, many small sea animals live there. Often sea animals, such as crabs, sea urchins and shrimps, shelter under boulders. Some sea animals, such as boring clams or tube worms, burrow into the rocky boulders.

≋ At low tide, reef flats and boulder zones look dead, but they are not. The plants and animals living there are waiting for the tide to return so they can come out of hiding.

Beaches can be either sandy or rocky. This one is sandy.

Reef flats are gently sloping areas next to the beach.

Boulder zones have many large dead coral boulders.

Christmas tree worms

Christmas tree worms have segmented bodies like earthworms. They make small, chalky tubes on the surface of coral boulders. As the hard corals grow around the tubes, the Christmas tree worms grow. They can grow up to 50 or 60 millimeters (two to 2.5 inches) long. Christmas tree worms feed on tiny animals floating in the water. They catch their food by using their feathery tentacles to sense movement and changes in light levels. If Christmas tree worms are disturbed, they hide inside their tubes and close the entrance with a tiny plate.

Chitons

Chitons (say: kite-ons) are a group of snails that have eight plates in their shell held together by a circle of leathery flesh. They wander over rocky surfaces eating tiny seaweeds.

≋ Christmas tree worms can be easily seen on coral reefs because they are so brightly colored.

Did you know?
Early explorers thought that chitons looked like they were wearing armor and called them 'coat-of-mail' snails. Chitons became prized in explorers' collections because they looked so unusual.

≋ Chitons are the oldest group of sea snails on Earth.

Reef crests

Reef crests are parts of coral reefs. They are smooth flat zones between boulder zones and reef edges. Waves from open oceans crash onto these areas, smashing coral boulders and leaving the areas bare. Few animals and plants are able to live here. One plant that is able to live on reef crests is a reddish-colored seaweed called coralline **algae** (say: ko-ra-line al-gee). It grows on broken coral boulders and holds them together to form hard pavements. Without these hard pavements to protect them, other parts of coral reefs would be destroyed by waves.

≋ Deep coral pools form on reef crests because waves break parts of the hard pavements. Coral pools provide shelter from the rough ocean for many different plants and animals.

Reef edges are where coral reefs finish and open oceans begin.

Flat reef crests are easily seen at low tide.

Clownfish

Clownfish belong to a group of fishes called damselfish. They are brightly colored reef fish. Some are orange with white stripes. Others are pink with white stripes. Clownfish live between the stinging tentacles of anemones. Anemones do not sting clownfish because the fish are covered with slime made by the anemones' tentacles. The anemone senses that the clownfish are part of itself and does not sting them. If the clownfish leave for a day or so, the anemones' slime wears off. When the clownfish return, the anemone does not recognize them and stings them.

Clownfish benefit from living with anemones because they are protected from other animals by the anemones' stinging tentacles. Anemones also benefit from living with clownfish in two ways: firstly, anemones are cleaned by clownfish and secondly, anemones eat the leftovers from the clownfishes' food. This type of relationship between two living things is called symbiosis (say: sim-by-o-sis). Symbiosis means that both things benefit from living together.

≋ Clownfish live with anemones in deep coral pools where they are protected from rough ocean waves.

Did you know?
Reef crests can be 200 to 300 meters (656 to 984 feet) wide on some coral reefs in the Great Barrier Reef.

Reef edges

Reef edges are parts of coral reefs. They are the boundaries between coral reefs and open oceans. Just beyond reef edges are big colonies of living corals, such as branching staghorns and flat plate corals. They are able to grow so big because they are sheltered from breaking waves by the reef edges. As well, hundreds of different types of fishes swim about in shoals just beyond the reef edges. Other types of animals, such as cuttlefish and nudibranchs, also live beyond the reef edges.

≋ This picture shows many different types of damselfishes living on a reef edge. Some feed on tiny sea animals floating in the water. Others feed on tiny animals from the sea floor. Male damselfishes guard nests of eggs for two to seven days until they hatch.

Cuttlefish

Cuttlefish, along with squid and octopuses, belong to a group of animals called cephalopods (say: se-fa-lo-podz). Cuttlefish have 10 tentacles.

Cuttlefish have a fin running around the center of their body which helps them to swim slowly and to steer. They have eyes that see very much like human eyes. They are able to change their color quickly, which lets them blend into the background, protecting them from being eaten by other animals.

Cuttlefish have one bony plate inside their body which is called a cuttlebone. Cuttlebones are often found washed up on beaches.

Nudibranchs

Nudibranchs, or sea slugs, are snails that do not have shells. There are more than 400 different types of nudibranchs. Most are poisonous. They come in a variety of shapes and sizes and many are very brightly colored. Their bright colours may warn other animals that they are poisonous.

≋ Cuttlefish change color, squirt ink and swim away very quickly if they are in danger from other animals.

Did you know?
Cuttlebones are often put in bird cages for the birds to trim their beaks on.

≋ The bright colors of nudibranchs may warn other animals that they are poisonous if eaten.

Environment watch

Why are coral reefs important?

Coral reefs are important for many reasons. One reason is that they are balanced communities where animals and plants breed, grow, feed and live for their whole lives. Another reason is that coral reefs are beautiful places. We must all work together to ensure that coral reefs have a future.

Things You Can Do
to help protect coral reefs

◇ Be interested in what is happening to coral reefs around the world. Read the newspapers, watch the news and use the Internet to find out what is going on.

◇ Become involved and find out what governments, scientists, communities and you can do to help protect and conserve coral reefs.

◇ Adopt the 'four Rs'—Reduce, Reuse, Recycle, Rethink. Remember, rain and waste water cause litter and household waste to be washed into drains and then into oceans that contain coral reefs.

When you visit a coral reef:

◇ Take photographs and keep a diary of all the interesting plants and animals you see.

◇ Be careful where you walk, so you do not break or damage corals.

◇ If you pick up any living thing, make sure you put it back exactly where you found it.

◇ If you move a coral boulder, put it back in the same place, because small reef animals use it for shelter.

≋ Part of the Great Barrier Reef

Glossary

algae	plants, such as seaweeds, without leaves, stems or roots that live in wet conditions
asexual reproduction	when living things divide in half to make two new living things
atolls	coral reefs that are shaped like rings or horseshoes
barrier reefs	coral reefs that form barriers between the mainland and open oceans
beaches	sandy or rocky areas lying next to the sea
boulder zones	parts of coral reefs made from large dead coral boulders, beyond reef flats
cays	low-lying islands made from sediments
continental islands	areas of high land on continental shelves, such as mountains or hills, that have become islands because the level of the sea has risen
continental shelves	sloping areas close to the mainland that are covered with shallow seawater
coral polyps	tiny sea animals related to anemones and jellyfish
coral reefs	rocky areas found in shallow, tropical water that have communities of plants and animals living on, in and around them
Equator	an imaginary line around the center of the Earth, where the sun is directly overhead at midday and the weather is very hot
fertilizer	food for plants
fringing reefs	coral reefs that form on continental shelves close to the mainland or continental islands
gut	the digestive tract, which includes the oesophagus, stomach and intestines
hard corals	corals that have skeletons
hermaphrodites	living things that have both female and male reproductive parts in their bodies
indigenous	the first people to live in a place or country
limestone	a rock made from the skeletons of dead sea animals, especially hard corals
nutrients	chemicals in the environment that living things need to grow
oceans	large bodies of salt water
reef crests	parts of coral reefs that are smooth, flat zones just before reef edges
reef edges	places where coral reefs finish and open oceans begin
reef flats	parts of coral reefs lying off beaches
sexual reproduction	when an egg and a sperm from living things blend together to make new living things
soft corals	corals that do not have skeletons
tropics	the area on the Earth between the Tropic of Cancer and the Tropic of Capricorn where the temperatures are always warm or hot
zooxanthellae	tiny plants that live inside the bodies of coral polyps

Index